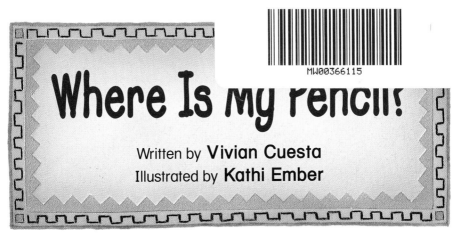

Where Is my Pencil?

Written by **Vivian Cuesta**

Illustrated by **Kathi Ember**

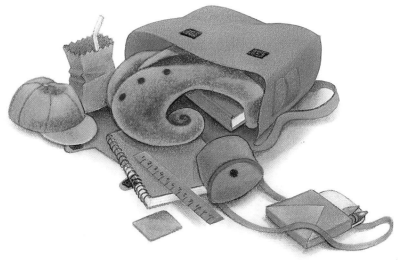

Celebration Press

An Imprint of Pearson Learning

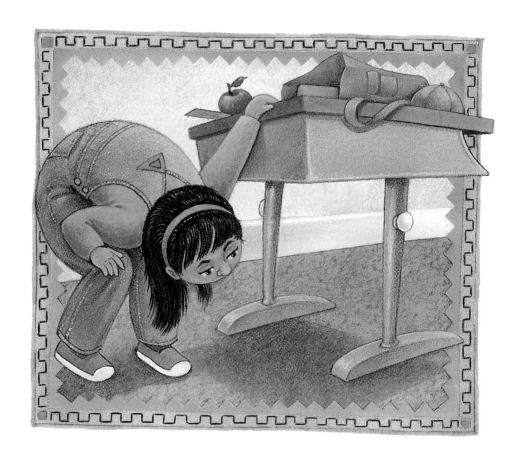

Is it under my desk?

Is it under my chair?

Is it under my book?

4

Is it under my crayons?

Is it under my notebook?

Is it under my paper?

Where is my pencil?